The month of May, from the illuminated manuscript
Les Très Riches Heures du duc de Berry

The Story of a Special Day
Volume 127

May

6

126th day of the year
(127th in leap years)
239 days remaining
until the end of the year.

by Michael Dobson

Timespinner
Press

This book is also available in e-book form for Kindle, e-
pub devices, and other formats from your favorite online
booksellers.

For more information about the series, about us, or about
your special day, please email us at
editor@timespinnerpress.com.

Look for other volumes in *The Story of a Special Day*,
coming often. See www.timespinnerpress.com for details
and for the most recent information.

Table of Contents

Cover: The *Hindenburg* disaster, May 6, 1937 — the *Event of the Day.*

Back Cover and Frontispiece: The month of May, from the French Gothic illuminated manuscript *Les Très Riches Heures du duc de Berry.*

May 6 Quotations

"The art of leadership is saying no, not yes. It is very easy to say yes."

—Tony Blair, born May 6, 1953

"I believe that dreams — day dreams, you know, with your eyes wide open and your brain machinery whizzing — are likely to lead to the betterment of the world."

—L. Frank Baum, died May 6, 1919

"In Italy, for thirty years under the Borgias, they had warfare, terror, murder and bloodshed - they produced Michelangelo, Leonardo Da Vinci and the Renaissance. In Switzerland, they had brotherly love and five hundred years of democracy and peace, and what did they produce? The cuckoo clock!"

—Orson Welles, born May 6, 1915

"It is not enough to be industrious; so are the ants. What are you industrious about?"

—Henry David Thoreau, died May 6, 1862

"Being entirely honest with oneself is a good exercise."

—Sigmund Freud, born May 6, 1856

Event of the Day
Hindenberg Disaster

LZ 129 *Hindenburg* at Lakehurst Naval Air Station, 1936

Unmanned balloons date back to 220 CE, but it was not until 1783 that the Montgolfier brothers made the first recorded manned balloon flight.

Balloons are dependent on the wind, so the race began to develop a steerable balloon, known as airships or dirigibles. In 1785, Jean-Pierre Blanchard crossed the English Channel in a balloon equipped with flapping wings and a bird-like tail. In 1852, Henri Giffard flew 17 miles (27 km) is a steam-powered airship.

In 1874, German Count Ferdinand von Zeppelin eveloped a plan to create an airship with a rigid structure that would be filled with smaller balloons, known as cells. (Blimps, or non-rigid airships, use only a single envelope to contain the lifting gas.)

In 1900, he flew his first airship, LZ 1, and by 1910, the world's first airline, DELAG, offered regular Zeppelin service between German cities. The Germans used Zeppelins in World War I both for observation and for bombing.

By the 1930s, Zeppelins provided regular transatlantic service to North America and Brazil. LZ 127 *Graf Zeppelin* made 590 flights and traveled over a million miles between 1928 and 1937, including an around-the-world trip. DELAG at that time had a perfect safety record, with no injuries or fatalities in all its long years of operation.

Airships of that period primarily used flammable hydrogen rather than inert helium. While hydrogen was easily available worldwide, the world's primary supply of helium was located in the United States, which restricted its export.

The largest of the Zeppelins, LZ 129 *Hindenburg*, was designed to use helium, but the U.S. unwillingness to sell helium to Germany forced it to use hydrogen as its lifting gas.

The *Hindenburg* was named for Weimar era German president Paul von Hindenburg, although Nazi propaganda minister Joseph Goebbels demanded it be renamed *Adolf Hitler*. When the Zeppelin company refused, Goebbels had a swastika painted on *Hindenburg*'s tail.

The *Hindenburg* was massive. Over 800 feet (245 meters) long, it carried seven million cubic feet of hydrogen. Its four Daimler-Benz diesel engines gave it a cruising speed of 85 mph (135 km/h).

Hindenburg entered commercial service in 1936. In its first year, it made 17 transatlantic round trips to New York and Rio, flying nearly 200,000 miles and carrying nearly 3,000 passengers. All that ended on its second transatlantic flight of the 1937 season.

Hindenburg left Frankfurt for New Jersey's Lakehurst Naval Air Station on May 3, 1937, reaching North America three days later. Thunderstorms passing over Lakehurst delayed the airship's arrival by a few hours, but at 7:00pm it was cleared for final approach. At 7:21pm, at an altitude of 650 feet (200 meters) above the ground, *Hindenburg* released landing lines that would be used by ground handlers to tether the airship to its mooring mast.

Four minutes later, at 7:25pm, disaster struck. Flames appeared on the port side near the fin, then spread to the top. People on board heard a muffled explosion.

In seconds, the flames engulfed the entire ship. In slightly more than half a minute, the *Hindenburg* was destroyed, although diesel fuel continued to burn for several hours.

Of the 36 passengers and 61 crewmembers on board, most survived. Thirteen passengers, 22 crew members, and one member of the ground crew perished, for a total of 36 killed.

A number of newsreel photographers were covering the landing, as the opening of *Hindenburg*'s travel season was big news. In particular, the radio broadcast of Herbert Morrison became the most famous account of the disaster:

"It's burst into flames! Get this, Charlie; get this, Charlie! It's fire... and it's crashing! It's crashing terrible! Oh, my! ... It's burning and bursting into flames and the... and it's falling on the mooring mast. And all the folks agree that this is terrible; this is the worst of the worst catastrophes in the world. [indecipherable] its flames... Crashing, oh! Four- or five-hundred feet into the sky and it... it's a terrific crash, ladies and gentlemen. It's smoke, and it's in flames now; and the frame is crashing to the ground, not quite to the mooring mast. Oh, the humanity!"

To this day, the exact location and cause of the initial fire remains controversial. Some sources have argued for sabotage, but no confirming proof has ever been found. Other suggested causes include a static spark, a lightning strike, engine failure, incendiary paint, a hydrogen leak, a gasbag puncture, structural failure, and an engine fuel leak. All remain unconfirmed.

The *Hindenburg* disaster, along with improvements in heavier-than-air travel, doomed the airship passenger industry, although some airships, such as the famous Goodyear blimp, continue to operate today.

There is a memorial at the *Hindenburg* crash site, and there are a number of films, books, and other media presentations of the disaster. As of 2012, two survivors of the disaster were still alive.

May 6 Holidays and Celebrations

Day of Bravery (Bulgaria)

The Bulgarian Day of Bravery is celebrated each year on May 6, the Feast of St. George, who is the patron saint of the Bulgarian Army.

Đurđevdan (Ђурђевдан) (Bosnia, Bulgaria, Croatia, Roma, Serbia)

In Orthodox (Eastern) Christianity, St. George is one of the most important Christian saints, and is the patron saint of warriors for Slavs, Georgians Circassians, Cossacks, Chetniks, and others. Celebrations of Đurđevdan ("George's Day") mark the return of springtime. People decorate their homes with flowers and twigs, grill lambs, and wash with water from church wells. It is similar to the Turkish celebration of Hıdırellez.

Hıdırellez (Turkey)

The religious celebration of Hıdırellez marks the day that the Prophet Hızır (الخضر), a figure in Islam said to have been a contemporary of Moses or Abraham, met the Prophet Elijah (אֵלִיָּהוּ in Hebrew, إلياس in Arabic), who is revered in Islam as in Judaism and Christianity.

Hızır is also associated with the Christian St. George, and is believed by Muslims to be the same person. Hıdırellez celebrations begin the evening of May 5 and continue through May 6. The holiday is also celebrated in other countries throughout the Middle East and the Balkans. Rituals include jumping over the Hıdırellez fire and bathing in water from a holy place. There is a superstition that all wishes and prayers made on this day will come true.

International No Diet Day (International)

International No Diet Day celebrates body acceptance and body shape diversity, and promotes a healthy life style at any size. It is observed on May 6 and is symbolized by a light blue ribbon.

Martyr's Day (Syria and Lebanon)

A national holiday in Syria and Lebanon, Martyr's Day commemorates the May 6, 1916, public execution of Arab nationalists by Djemal Pasha (جمال باشا), part of the leading triumvirate of the Ottoman Empire.

Teacher's Day (Jamaica)

Many nations around the world honor teachers on a special day. In Jamaica, it is observed on May 6, with most schools closing early.

Orthodox Bulgarian Icon of St. George fighting the dragon, for
Đurđevdan, Hıdırellez, and Yuri's Day

Yuri's Day in the Spring (Юрьев день) (Jamaica)

The Russian Orthodox Church celebrates the feast of St. George (Yuri in Russian) in the spring on May 6 and again on December 9.

Christian Feast Days

In **Western Christianity**, May 6 is the feast day of Dominic Savio, Evodius of Antioch, Gerard of Lunel, Lucius of Cyrene, and Petronax of Monte Cassino.

In **Eastern Orthodox Christianity**, May 6 is the Feast of St. George. (This feast is celebrated on April 23 in western Christianity, which uses the Gregorian calendar. This corresponds to May 6 in the Julian calendar, used in eastern Christianity for religious observances.) It is also the commemoration of Job the Long-Suffering; Saints Mamas, Pachomius, and Hilarion; Saint Lucius of Cyrene; Saint Vladimir II Monomakh; Saint Seraphim of Mt. Domvu; Saint Job of Pochaev; and Saint Sophia of Cleisoura. (These events are observed on May 19 by "Old Calendarists.")

What Happened on May 6?

1527 CE – **Sack of Rome**

On May 6, 1527, mutinous troops of Holy Roman Emperor Charles V attacked the city of Rome. Churches, monasteries, and palaces were ransacked, looted, and burned. Pope Clement VII was forced to surrender and pay 400,000 ducats for his life, as well as surrender many of the Papal domains to the Holy Roman Empire. The population of Rome dropped from 55,000 to 10,000 as a result of the sack.

Historians often cite this date as the end of the Italian Renaissance. Although Italy went into decline, the Renaissance spread into northern Europe. Commemorating this event, recruits to the Swiss Guard are sworn in each year on May 6.

1840 CE – **First Adhesive Postage Stamp**

The English Penny Black postage stamp, the world's first adhesive stamp used in a public postal system, went into official use on May 6, 1840. Previously, it was normal for the recipient to pay for a letter on delivery; with the Penny Black the sender could pre-pay postage. It was only used for a little over a year because the red cancellation stamp was hard to see, meaning that the stamps could be re-used.

An 1840 Penny Black stamp

1844 CE – **First Ice Skating Rink**

London's Glaciarium was the world's first ice rink using mechanically frozen ice. It opened on Monday, May 6, 1844, and continued in service until 1876.

1861 CE – **Richmond Becomes the Capital of the Confederacy**

On May 6, 1861, Richmond, Virginia, was declared the new capital of the Confederate States of America, replacing Montgomery, Alabama.

1863 CE – **Battle of Chancellorsville**

From April 30 to May 6, 1683, Union forces commanded by General Joseph Hooker faced a much smaller Confederate force led by General Robert E. Lee near the village of Chancellorsville, Virginia. A combination of audacity on the part of Lee and timidity on the part of Hooker led to a major Confederate victory, tempered by the death of General Stonewall Jackson from friendly fire.

1889 CE – **Eiffel Tower Opens**

On May 6, 1889, the Eiffel Tower opened to the public as part of the 1889 *Exposition Universelle* (Paris World's Fair). It was highly controversial in its day, but became a beloved symbol of the city of Paris. The most visited paid monument in the world, the Eiffel Tower was at the time of its construction the tallest man-made object in the world, surpassing the Washington Monument, and remained the record holder for 41 years, until it was surpassed by New York City's Chrysler Building.

1941 CE – **First Flight of the P-47 Thunderbolt**

The Republic P-47 Thunderbolt, which first flew on May 6, 1941, was one of the main fighter aircraft of World War II. Designed for the U.S. Army Air Force, it also flew for France, Britain, Russia, Mexico, and Brazil. When used as a fighter-bomber, it could carry over half the bomb weight of a B-17. It served in both the European and Pacific Theaters.

Poster for the Exposition Universelle, featuring the Eiffel Tower

1941 CE – **Bob Hope's First USO Show**

Beginning a tradition that would last over fifty years, entertainer Bob Hope performed his first USO show on May 6, 1941, at March Field, California. He continued to perform USO tours for the remainder of World War II, the Korean War, the Vietnam War, the Lebanese Civil War, the Iran-Iraq War, and the Persian Gulf War. He was named an "Honorary Veteran" by a 1997 act of Congress for his services.

Bob Hope entertains troops at a USO show

1954 CE – **Four-Minute Mile**

On May 6, 1954, English former Olympian Roger Bannister became the first person to break the "four-minute mile barrier," completing his run in 3 minutes, 59.4 seconds. While his record lasted only 46 days, it marked an important milestone in the history of running, and Bannister was named the first *Sports Illustrated* Sportsman of the Year for his achievement.

1960 CE – **Marriage of Princess Margaret**

In the first royal wedding to be broadcast on television, Princess Margaret, younger sister of Queen Elizabeth II and daughter of King George V, married photographer Antony Armstrong-Jones at Westminster Abbey on May 6, 1960. Over 300 million people worldwide viewed the televised wedding, The marriage ended in divorce after eighteen years.

1981 CE – **Design of the Vietnam Veterans Memorial Chosen**

On May 6, 1981, a jury of eight architects and sculptors unanimously selected a design for the Vietnam Veterans Memorial by Yale architectural student Maya Ying Lin out of 1,421 entries. While the choice was highly controversial at the time, referred to as a "black gash of shame," it has become a very popular symbol for veterans of the war. There are five privately financed traveling replicas of the War, as well as three fixed replicas in New Jersey, Kansas, and California.

1989 CE – **First Hypercoaster**

The Magnum XL-200, a steel roller coaster at Cedar Point Amusement Park in Sandusky, Ohio, entered the Guinness Book of World Records on its opening on May 6, 1989, as the tallest (205 feet), fastest (72 mph), and steepest (60°) complete-circute roller coaster in the world. Named the first "hypercoaster," it began the "roller coaster wars," a competition among amusement parks to build higher and faster roller coasters.

1994 CE – **Channel Tunnel Opens**

On May 6, 1994, Queen Elizabeth II of England and President François Mitterrand of France formally opened the Channel Tunnel, linking England and France by rail for the first time. The Tunnel stretches for 23.5 miles (37.9 kilometers) and has the longest undersea portion of any tunnel in the world.

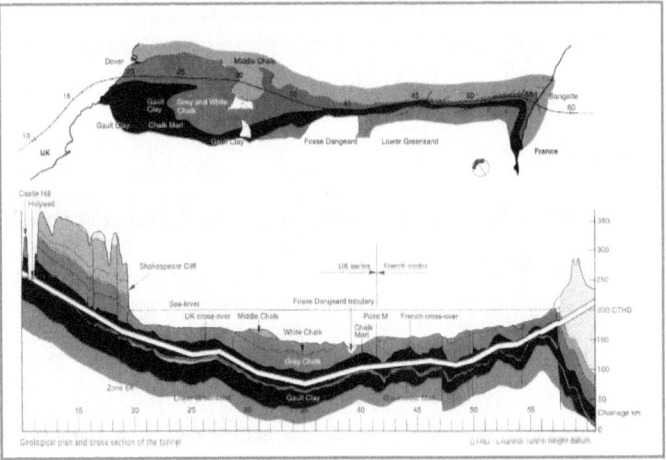

Geological profile of the Channel Tunnel

1994 CE – **Paula Jones Sues Bill Clinton**

On May 6, 1994, former Arkansas state employee Paula Jones sued U.S. President Bill Clinton for sexual harrassment. The lawsuit was dismissed before trial because Jones failed to demonstrate any damages. Jones appealed, but Clinton entered into an out-of-court settlement. The case is most notable because of statements made in depositions by Clinton concerning his relationship with White House intern Monica Lewinsky, which led to the impeachment of Clinton by the Republican-controlled U.S. House of Representatives.

1996 CE – **CIA Director's Body Found**

On May 6, 1996, former CIA director William Colby's body was found in the Wimlico River in Maryland, nine days after he left his weekend home on a late night solo canoe trip. The coroner determined that the death was accidental and resulted from drowning. Speculation that the death was the result of either murder or suicide continues, but no formal evidence has been found to cause an official reassessment.

1998 CE – **Kerry Wood Strikes Out Twenty Houston Astros**

On May 6, 1998, in his fifth career start, Chicago Cubs pitcher Kerry Wood tied Roger Clemens' record for strikeouts in a nine-inning game, throwing a one-hit, no walk, 20-strikeout shutouts against the Houston Astros.

Who Was Born on May 6?

Crime

Andreas Baader (May 6, 1943 — October 18, 1977)

German Andreas Baader was one of the leaders of the Baader-Meinhof Gang, also known as the Red Army Faction. He was arrested in 1972 and committed suicide in prison in 1977.

Rubin "Hurricane" Carter (May 6, 1937 —)

Middleweight boxer Rubin Carter's (right) conviction for homicide was overturned twice. He was the subject of Bob Dylan's song "Hurricane" and the 1999 film *The Hurricane*.

Martha Beck (May 6, 1920 — March 8, 1951)

Martha Beck and her partner Raymond Fernandez were known as the "Lonely Hearts Killers," who killed as many as 20 women between 1947 and 1949. The films The Honeymoon Killers, Deep Crimson, and Lonely Hearts were all based on this case. Both Beck and Fernandez were at Sing Sing prison by the electric chair.

Exploration

Robert Peary (May 6, 1856 — February 20, 1920)

U.S. Navy Rear Admiral Robert Peary claimed to have led the first successful expedition to the geographic North Pole, but later evidence suggests that he did not (though he may have come close).

Film and Television

Gabourey Sidibe (May 6, 1983 —)

Sidibe was nominated for an Academy Award for her acting debut in the 2009 film *Precious*.

Leslie Hope (May 6, 1965 —)

Hope played Teri Bauer in the TV series 24.

Robert Peary

George Clooney (May 6, 1961 —)

George Clooney (below) received three Golden Globe Awards and two Academy Awards. He gained fame on the TV series *ER*, and starred in numerous films including the *Ocean's Eleven* franchise, *Syriana*, *Confessions of a Dangerous Mind*, *Up in the Air*, and others. He is the only person to have been nominated for Academy Awards in six different categories.

Anne Parillaud (May 6, 1960 —)

Parillaud played the lead character in the 1990 French film *La Femme Nikita*.

Roma Downey (May 6, 1960 —)

Downey played Monica on the TV series *Touched by an Angel*.

Tom Bergeron (May 6, 1955 —)

Bergeron hosted the TV shows *Dancing With the Stars, America's Funniest Home Videos,* and *Hollywood Squares*.

Michael O'Hare (May 6, 1952 — September 28, 2012)

O'Hare is best known for his role as Commander Sinclair in the TV series *Babylon 5*.

Adriana Caselotti (May 6, 1916 — January 18, 1997)

Caselotti is best known as the voice of the title character in Disney's *Snow White and the Seven Dwarfs*.

Orson Welles (May 6, 1915 — October 10, 1985)

Actor, director, writer, and producer Orson Welles is remembered for his 1941 film *Citizen Kane*, ranked as one of the greatest movies of all time, for his radio broadcast of *The War of the Worlds*, and for many other films including *The Magnificent Ambersons*, *Touch of Evil*, and *The Third Man*.

Orson Welles in *Citizen Kane* (1941)

Stewart Granger (May 6, 1913 — August 16, 1993)

Actor Stewart Granger was known for his heroic and romantic leading roles. His films included *King Solomon's Mines*, *The Prisoner of Zenda*, and *North to Alaska*. He replaced Lee J. Cobb as the ranch owner on TV's *The Virginian*.

Frank Nelson (May 6, 1911 — September 12, 1986)

Comic actor Nelson was best known for his catchphrase "EEE-Yeeeeeesssss?" He made more than 10,000 television appearances.

Raymond Bailey (May 6, 1904 — April 15, 1980)

Actor Raymond Bailey is best remembered for playing banker Milburn Drysdale in *The Beverly Hillbillies.*

Max Ophüls (May 6, 1902 — March 26, 1957)

German-born film director Ophüls made over 30 films, including the Oscar-nominated *Le Plaisir.*

Rudolph Valentino (May 6, 1895 — August 23, 1926)

Known as the "Latin Lover," Rudolph Valentino (next page) was a major sex symbol in the silent film era, known particularly for his role in *The Sheik.* When he died at age 31, over 100,000 people tried to attend his funeral.

Rudoph Valentino and Agnes Ayres in *The Sheik* (1921)

Medicine

Sigmund Freud (May 6, 1856 — September 23, 1939)

Viennese neurologist Sigmund Freud (right) developed the discipline of psychoanalysis. One of the most important, influential, and controversial figures in the treatment of mental illness, his ideas and concepts continue to figure prominently throughout the fields of psychology and psychiatry.

Music

Mary MacGregor (May 6, 1948 —)

MacGregor is known for her 1976 hit "Torn Between Two Lovers."

Bob Seger (May 6, 1945 —)

Bob Seger's hit songs include "Night Moves," "Against the Wind," and "Old Time Rock and Roll." He was inducted into the Songwriter's Hall of Fame in 2012.

Billy Cotton (May 6, 1899 — March 25, 1969)

British bandleader Billy Cotton was known as a 1950s and 1960s radio and television personality in the UK.

Politics and Society

Tony Blair (May 6, 1953 —)

Tony Blair was Prime Minister of the United Kingdom from 1997 to 2007.

Samuel Doe (May 6, 1899 — March 25, 1969)

Samuel Doe became President of Liberia in a 1980 coup, and ruled the country until his 1990 assassination. He was the first indigenous head of state in Liberian history.

Patricia Kennedy Lawford (May 6, 1924 — September 17, 2006)

Sister of President John F. Kennedy, Patricia Kennedy Lawford married actor Peter Lawford in 1954; they divorced in 1966.

Maximilien de Robespierre (May 6, 1758 — July 28, 1794)

French lawyer and politician Robespierre was a leading figure in the French Revolution. He was part of the Committee of Public Safety as it carried out the Reign of Terror, in which over 40,000 people were executed in a series of political purges. He was eventually arrested and executed by guillotine.

Robespierre by Pierre Roch Vigneron

Restauranteurs

Jilly Rizzo (May 6, 1917 — May 6, 1992)

Rizzo operated Jilly's Saloon in New York, a popular celebrity hangout in the 1960s patronized by Frank Sinatra, among others, and appeared numerous times on *Rowan and Martin's Laugh-In*. He was born and died on the same day.

Toots Shor (May 6, 1903 — January 23, 1977)

Toots Shor's famous New York City restaurants were known for the large number of celebrities who dined there. He was known for his witty jibes poking fun at his celebrity guests, ranging from movie executive Louis B. Mayer to Frank Sinatra. He often said he didn't care if he was a millionaire — as long as he could live like one.

Sports

Chris Paul (May 6, 1985 —)

Basketball player Chris Paul was NBA Rookie of the Year, an All-Star MVP, and part of two gold medal-winning US Olympic basketball teams. He played for the New Orleans Hornets and Los Angeles Clippers.

Kyle Shewfelt (May 6, 1982 —)

Canadian gymnast Shewfelt won a gold medal in the floor exercise event in the 2004 Athens Olympics.

Colt Cabana (May 6, 1980 —)

Wrestler Scott Colton was World Heavyweight Champion five times.

John Abraham (May 6, 1978 —)

Defensive end Abraham played for the University of South Carolina, the New York Jets, and the Atlanta Falcons, becoming a member of the 100 Sacks Club.

Naoko Takahashi (高橋 尚子) (May 6, 1972 —)

Takahashi won gold in the 2000 Sydney Olympics women's marathon, holding the women's record from then until 2012.

Martin Brodeur (May 6, 1972 —)

Ice hockey goaltender Brodeur is the all-time NHL leader in regular season wins, with three Stanley Cups and two Olympic gold medals.

Masanori Murakami (村上 雅則) (May 6, 1944 —)

San Francisco Giants pitcher Mashi Murakami was the first Japanese player to play for a Major League team.

Willie Mays (May 6, 1931 —)

Known as the "Say Hey Kid," Willie Mays was ranked second on *The Sporting News* List of the 100 Greatest Baseball Players. He played for the New York/San Francisco Giants and the New York Mets, and was elected to the Baseball Hall of Fame in 1979, his first year of eligibility.

Willie Mays

Harry Watson (May 6, 1923 — November 19, 2002)

Ice hockey left wing Watson's teams won five Stanley Cups. He was inducted into the Hockey Hall of Fame in 1994.

Weeb Ewbank (May 6, 1907 — November 17, 1998)

Pro Football Hall of Fame coach Weeb Ewbank led the New York Jets to victory over the Baltimore Colts in Super Bowl III.

Writing

Theodore H. White (May 6, 1915 — May 15, 1986)

Journalist and historian Theodore H. White is known for his *The Making of the President* series, covering the 1960, 1964, 1968, 1972, and 1980 elections.

Harry Golden (May 6, 1902 — October 2, 1981)

Jewish-American journalist and publisher Harry Golden was known for his outspoken opposition to segregation as a reporter for the Charlotte (North Carolina) *Observer*, and for his best-selling book *For 2¢ Plain*.

Who Died on May 6?

Education

Maria Montessori (August 31, 1870 — May 6, 1952)

Italian physician and educator Montessori developed the Montessori method of education, used widely today.

Film and Television

George Lindsey (December 17, 1928 — May 6, 2012)

Lindsey (right) was best known for playing Goober Pyle on *The Andy Griffith Show* and for his continuing role on *Hee-Haw*.

Marlene Dietrich (December 27, 1901 — May 6, 1992)

Dietrich gained fame for her role in 1930's *The Blue Angel,* and starred in such films as *Destry Rides Again* and *Shanghai Express.*

Marlene Dietrich

Wilfrid Hyde-White (May 12, 1903 — May 6, 1991)

Hyde-White had an extensive stage career and is best known to American audiences for his role as Colonel Pickering in the 1964 film of *My Fair Lady*.

Monty Wooley (August 17, 1888 — May 6, 1963)

Actor Monty Woolley (below) is best known for his role in *The Man Who Came to Dinner*. His trademark was his distinctive white beard.

Letters

L. Frank Baum (May 15, 1856 — May 6, 1919)

Children's author L. Frank Baum's best known work is *The Wizard of Oz*. He wrote 55 novels and numerous other works, including thirteen more Oz books.

Promotional poster for *The Wizard of Oz* (1900)

Bret Harte (August 25, 1836 — May 6, 1902)

California author Bret Harte's well known works include "The Outcasts of Poker Flats."

Henry David Thoreau (July 12, 1817 — May 6, 1862)

Philosopher, author, and transcendentalist Henry David Thoreau (below) is known for such works as *Walden* and *Civil Disobedience.*

Music

Otis Blackwell (February 16, 1931— May 6, 2002)

Songwriter Otis Blackwell's well-known compositions include "Great Balls of Fire, "Don't Be Cruel," "All Shook Up," "Return to Sender," and "Handy Man."

Ted Weems (September 26, 1901 — May 6, 1963)

Bandleader and musician Ted Weems led a popular big band. His hits include "Somebody Stole My Gal," "Heartaches," and "I Wonder Who's Kissing Her Now" with Perry Como.

Politics

William J. Casey (March 13, 1913 — May 6, 1987)

Casey was Director of Central Intelligence from 1981 to 1987.

Edward VII (November 9, 1841 — May 6, 1910)

British King Edward VII was heir to Queen Victoria and father of King George V. He was Prince of Wales for a longer period than any of his predecessors during the reign of his mother.

Religion

József Mindszenty (March 29, 1892 — May 6, 1975)

Cardinal and leader of the Catholic Church in Hungary, Mindszenty was imprisoned by the Nazis and subsequently by the communists, tortured and given a life sentence, before being freed in 1956 and granted political asylum by the United States.

François de Laval (October 28, 1585 — May 6, 1638)

First Roman Catholic bishop of Quebec, de Laval is known as the Father of the Canadian Church. He is currently a candidate for sainthood.

Cornelius Jansen (October 28, 1585 — May 6, 1638)

Catholic bishop of Ypres, Jansen inspired a theological movement known as Jansenism, later condemned as heretical by Pope Innocent X.

Science

Theodore von Kármán (May 11, 1881 — May 6, 1963)

Hungarian-American mathematician and aerospace engineer is regarded as the outstanding aerodynamic theoretician of the 20th century. His work in supersonic and hypersonic airflow underlies many modern developments in flight.

Alexander von Humboldt (September 14, 1769 — May 6, 1859)

Naturalist and explorer Alexander von Humboldt's work in botanical geography established a foundation for the field of biogeography. His name is given to numerous plants, geographical features, and universities.

Sports

Robin Roberts (September 20, 1926 — May 6, 2010)

Baseball Hall of Fame member Robin Roberts pitched for the Philadelphia Phillies for the majority of his major league career.

Art Houtteman (August 17, 1888 — May 6, 1963)

Houtteman played 12 seasons in Major League Baseball for the Detroit Tigers, Cleveland Indians, and Baltimore Orioles.

Earl Blaik (February 15, 1897 — May 6, 1989)

Red Blaik was head football coach at Dartmouth College and West Point. He was inducted into the College Football Hall of Fame in 1964.

May
The Fifth Month

"Then came fair May, the fairest maid on ground,
Deck'd all with dainties of the season's pride,
And throwing flowers out of her lap around. ."

— *Edward Spenser,* The Faerie Queene, *Book VII*

According to many scholars, the month of May takes its name from the Roman goddess Maia, an earth goddess who was the mother of Mercury. The poet Ovid, on the other hand, claimed that May took its name from the Latin *maiores*, meaning ancestors. In either case, the month of May in ancient Rome was marked by sacrifices to Maia, and her son Mercury was honored on the Ides of May (May 15).

May is the fifth month of the year in both Julian and Gregorian calendars. It was originally the third month in ancient Rome, because the new year began on March 1. Although Julius Caesar changed the length of several months during his great calendar reform (the Julian calendar), the length of May has remained constant at 31 days.

In the northern hemisphere, May occurs in the springtime, and in the southern hemisphere, May takes place in fall. Strangely, no other month begins or ends on the same day of the week as the beginning or ending of May, although January of the following year always begins and ends on the same day of the week as this year's May.

May in Other Cultures

In Latin and Old English, the month of May was named *Maius*, and it is *Mai* in French. In Arabic, the month is مايو, pronounced *māyū*. In Chinese, the equivalent month is 五月. Croatians call the month *svibanj* and in Czech it is *květen*. In Finland, it is *toukokuu*. The Jewish month of Sivan (סִיוָן) normally falls in May-June. It is the third month of the Jewish ecclesiastical year. The Irish called the month *bealtaine*, and it marked the beginning of summer. Slovenians call May *veliki traven*, or the month of the big grass.

May Superstitions

May is an unlucky month for getting married.

Never buy a broom in May.

"Wash a blanket in May / Wash a dear one away."

Cats born in May will bring snakes into the house.

"Those who bathe in May / Will soon be laid in clay."

May Symbols

Birthstone: Emerald

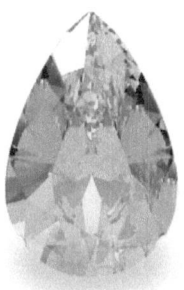

Birth Flowers: Lily of the Valley and Hawthorn.

Lily of the Valley   Common Hawthorn

May Events

Honorary Months

Presidents, Congresses, and nations around the world issue proclamations recognizing particular months to honor certain causes. These events generally fall in April. (All US unless otherwise noted.)

- American Bike Month
- Asian Pacific American Heritage Month
- Asparagus Month
- Jewish American Heritage Month
- Mental Heath Awareness Month
- Music Month (New Zealand)
- National ALS Awareness Month
- National Brain Tumor Awareness Month
- National Military Appreciation Month
- National Moving Month
- National Smile Month (United Kingdom)
- Older Americans Month
- Skin Cancer Awareness Month
- South Asian Heritage Month

Moveable and Multi-Day Events

Some events take place over a specific week or time period. Start and finish dates may vary from year to year. Some events occur on different days each year (such as "fourth Saturday of a month").

Kentucky Derby

The Kentucky Derby, a stakes race for three-year-old thoroughbred horses, is held on the first Saturday in May at Churchill Downs, Louisville, Kentucky. It is the first leg of the Triple Crown, which includes the Preakness and Belmont. It is known as "the most exciting two minutes in sports."

Military Spouse Day (United States)

On Military Spouse Day, the contributions and support of military spouses is honored. It is held on the Friday before Mother's Day. The earliest day it can occur is May 6; the latest is May 12.

Vesākha (वैशाख)

The Buddhist holiday day known as Vesākha or simply Vesak commemorates the birth, enlightenment, and death of Gautama Buddha. It is celebrated on the first full moon of the month of Vesākha, which normally falls in April or May, and in leap years in the month of June.

Easter (Eastern Christianity)

The Christian holiday of Easter, marking the resurrection of Jesus Christ, is celebrated on the first Sunday after the Paschal Full Moon following the March equinox, which is officially set at March 21 by church reckoning. In Western Christianity, that puts Easter somewhere between March 22 and April 25.

Because Eastern (Orthodox) Christianity uses the Julian calendar for religious purposes, Easter in that calendar can take place anywhere from April 4 to May 8. A number of religious events take place in the week before Easter, including Maundy Thursday and Good Friday. The week following Easter in Eastern Christianity is known as Bright Week, and continues the celebration of the resurrection in church services.

Easter Eggs

May Zodiac Signs

From the perspective of someone on Earth, the Sun appears to move through the sky throughout the year, along a path astronomers call the ecliptic plane. The ecliptic plane is divided into twelve constellations, known as the zodiac, based on traditionally observed patterns of stars. On your birthday, you can't see your constellation, because it's part of the daytime sky.

The zodiac was first developed by Babylonian astronomers about 2,500 years ago. Because they were unaware that the Earth wobbles like a spinning top (a motion known as *precession*), they didn't make allowance for the fact that the Sun's path through the zodiac changes over time.

That means there are now two sets of dates for your birth sign. The *tropical* dates are the original Babylonian dates; the *siderial* dates tell you where the Sun actually appears as it moves along its annual path.

In siderial reckoning, May 6 is in Aries, but in traditional tropical astrology, May 6 is in Taurus.

Aries

Tropical March 21 to April 19

Siderial April 15 to May 15

In Greek mythology, Aries is a ram with golden wings and golden wool who rescued the twins Phrixus and Helle from certain death. Although Helle died in the rescue attempt, the grateful Phrixus sacrificed the ram to Zeus. The golden fleece from the sacrificed ram played a prominent part in the later myth of Jason and the Argonauts.

In astrology, Aries, a fire sign, is compatible with the other fire signs of Gemini, Leo, and Sagittarius, and to a lesser extent with air signs Scorpio and Libra. Arians are supposed to be adventurous, enthusiastic, quick-tempered, and impulsive.

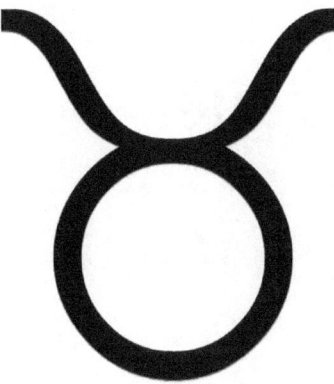

Taurus

Tropical April 21 to May 22

Siderial May 16 to June 15

In Greek mythology, Taurus was a disguise adopted by Zeus, who appeared to the maiden Europa in the form of a gentle white bull. Europa unwisely got too close, and Zeus kidnapped her to the island of Crete, where she bore him three sons, including Minos, builder of the labyrinth that housed the minotaur.

In astrology, Taurus is an earth sign, and Taureans are supposed to be quiet, gentle, compassionate, and stubborn. Taureans can appreciate the finer things in life and are cautious with money.

Illustration by Edward Penfield

What Day of the Week is May 6?

On what day of the week does May 6 fall?

Surprisingly, this isn't an easy question. Because the calendar year is 365 days long (366 in leap years), it doesn't divide evenly by the seven days of the week.

Also, the Earth goes around the Sun in about 365-1/4 days, so a calendar tends to drift over time. That's why the same date falls on different weekdays in different years.

This is made even more complicated by a change in calendars that took place in 1582. Our modern calendar has its roots in ancient Rome, in a calendar reform conducted by Julius Caesar. Caesar commissioned mathematicians to attack the problem, and they came up with the idea of *leap years*, and thus standardized the calendar for centuries to come. This was called the *Julian calendar*.

Over time, however, the small errors in Caesar's calculation compounded. That's why Pope Gregory XIII commissioned the *Gregorian calendar*, used in most of the world today. Some countries converted in 1582, when the calendar was first developed; some converted later; other still haven't changed.

Gregorian and Julian aren't the only types of calendars. The Hebrew year, the Islamic year, and many other calendars are used in different parts of the world and among different people.

You can convert Gregorian dates to other calendars, including the Hebrew calendar, the Islamic calendar, and even the Mayan calendar by visiting the Fourmilab Calendar Converter at http://www.fourmilab.ch/documents/calendar/.

Chinese calendar systems are quite complex and have changed several times; a full discussion is far beyond the scope of this book. If you're interested, you can find information here: http://www.hermetic.ch/cal_stud/chinese_cal.htm.

A 50-year brass perpetual calendar.

Copyright, Credit, and Contact

Follow Us

Our blog *Dobson's Improbable History* (http://improbhistory.blogspot.com) features short articles on events and people associated with each day, and updates several times each week. You can also get a daily "What Happened In History" message and all the latest Timespinner Press news by following us on Facebook at https://www.facebook.com/TimespinnerPress. Our Twitter feed @SidewiseThinker links you to all our News of the Day.

Contact Us

Find an error or a format problem? Want information about the series, about us, or about when the volume for your special day might be available? Please email us at editor@timespinnerpress.com. (We also take requests.)

On Dates

Historians use "CE" (Common Era) and "BCE" (Before the Common Era) instead of the more common "AD" (*Anno Domini*, or Year of Our Lord) and "BC" (Before Christ), reflecting the fact that the year-numbering system established by the Gregorian calendar is used throughout the world in many countries not culturally Christian.

The CE/BCE designation dates back to at least 1708, and have been adopted as a standard by the United Nations and the Universal Postal Union. Because this series of books covers events and people of all nations and cultures, we use the CE/BCE terms.

The abbreviation "O.S." on some dates refers to the fact that the Russian Empire did not switch from the Julian to the Gregorian calendar at the same time as the rest of Europe, and therefore some figures and events have two dates. (See "What Day of the Week…" for an explanation of Julian and Gregorian dates.)

People and events whose original names are not in the Western alphabet have their native names (where possible) in the appropriate script shown in parenthesis. If you are using an e-reader to access an electronic version of this book, all characters don't always display on all devices.

Sources and Art Credits

We owe a great debt to Wikipedia, which is our first stop for research. We attempt to make independent confirmation of all important dates and facts through a variety of other sources. Other sources we frequently use include the Library of Congress; "on this day" listings from *Encyclopedia Britannica*, the New York *Times*, and the BBC; and, of course, the always-useful Google.

All art and photographs are either in the public domain, used under a Creative Commons license, or with a "fair use" justification, and most frequently come from Wikimedia Commons and the Library of Congress Prints and Photographs Division.

Attribution is provided where requested by the copyright owner or when of historical significance, listed below. For information about any particular illustration or photograph, please contact us.

- The cover photograph of the *Hindenburg* disaster was taken by Gus Pasquarella of the U.S. Navy. It is in the public domain because it was taken in the course of his duties with the U.S. Navy.
- The illustration of the month of May used on the back cover and as the frontispiece is from the French Gothic illuminated manuscript *Les Très Riches Heures du duc de Berry* by the Limbourg Brothers, Jean Colombe, and an intermediate painter whose name is lost to history. It is in the public domain because its copyright has expired.
- The photograph of LZ 129 *Hindenburg* at the Lakehurst Naval Air Station was taken in 1936 by a sailor or employee of the U.S. Navy as part of that person's official duties and is thus in the public domain. Because the photograph contains a Nazi swastika, we add the following disclaimer: The purpose

of displaying this photograph is to report on the historically significant event of the *Hindenburg* disaster. Under Section 86a of the German criminal code, display of images containing Nazi symbols such as the swastika that are normally banned are legally permitted when the purpose is reporting about current historical events, per Section 86, subsection (3). The same justification is claimed under the criminal laws of other countries that ban the use and display of Nazi symbols.

- The Orthodox Bulgarian Icon of St. George fighting the dragon is from the 1621 *Book of Emblems* by Andrea Alciato. It is in the public domain because its copyright has expired.

- The photograph of the 1840 Penny Black stamp is in the public domain as a work of the Government of the United Kingdom created prior to 1963.

- The 1889 poster of the Paris Exposition Universelle is in the public domain because its copyright has expired.

- The 1944 photograph of Bob Hope entertaining soldiers is in the public domain as a work created by the U.S. federal government.

- The Channel Tunnel geological profile is by "Tambo" and used here under the CC BY-SA 3.0 license.

- The 1958 photograph of Rubin Carter was released into the public domain under the CC0 1.0 dedication.

- The 1909 photogravure of Robert Peary was taken by Benjamin B. Hampton. It is in the public domain because its copyright has expired.

- The 2009 photograph of George Clooney at the 66th Venice International Film Festival was taken by Nicolas Genin and is used here under the terms of the CC BY-SA 2.0 license.

- The 1941 promotional photograph of Orson Welles in *Citizen Kane* is in the public domain because it was originally distributed without a copyright notice, and if a copyright was later filed, it was not renewed.

- The 1921 photograph of Rudolph Valentino and Agnes Ayres in *The Sheik* is in the public domain because its copyright has expired.

- The 1922 photograph of Sigmund Freud is from the Google-hosted LIFE Photo Archive. It is in the public domain because its copyright has expired.

- The 1786 portrait of Maximilien Robespierre by Pierre Roch

Vigneron is in the public domain because its copyright has expired. The original is in the Palace of Versailles.

- The photograph of Willie Mays was on the front cover of the September 1954 issue of *Baseball Digest*. It is in the public domain because it was first published in the United States between 1923 and 1963 with a copyright notice, but the copyright was not renewed.

- The 1966 publicity photograph from *The Andy Griffith Show* is in the public domain because it was first published in the United States between 1923 and 1977 without a copyright notice.

- The publicity photograph of Marlene Dietrich from *Shanghai Express* is in the public domain because its copyright has expired.

- The publicity photograph of Monty Wooley in *The Man Who Came To Dinner* is in the public domain because it was first published in the United States between 1923 and 1977 without a copyright notice.

- The 1900 advertising poster for *The Wizard of Oz* is in the public domain because its copyright has expired.

- The 1856 daguerreotype of Henry David Thoreau by Benjamin D. Maxham is in the public domain because its copyright has expired. The original is in the collection of the Smithsonian Institution's National Portrait Gallery.

- The photograph of an emerald was taken by Les Facettes and is used here under the CC BY-SA 3.0 license.

- The photograph of a lily of the valley (*convallaria majalis*) is by H. Zell and is used here under the CC BY-SA 3.0 license.

- The photograph of a hawthorn (*Crataegus monogyna*) is by Sannse and is used here under the CC BY-SA 3.0 license.

- The photograph of Czechoslovakian Easter eggs was taken by Jan Kameníček, who has released the image into the public domain.

- The photograph of the 1906 automobile calendar by Edward Penfield is from the Library of Congress Prints and Photographs Division, and is in the public domain because it was published prior to January 1, 1923.

- The 50-year perpetual calendar photograph is in the public domain.

License Description and Terms

Aside from material purely in the public domain, photographs and other material in this book are used under specific licenses permitting free use, usually with attribution. For full text and terms of these licenses, click or enter the appropriate links below.

- Creative Commons Attribution 2.0 Generic (CC BY 2.0):: http://creativecommons.org/licenses/by/2.0/deed.en

- Creative Commons Attribution-Share Alike 3.0 Generic (CC BY-SA 3.0): http://creativecommons.org/licenses/by-sa/3.0/

- Creative Commons Attribution-Share Alike 2.5 Generic (CC BY-SA 2.5): http://creativecommons.org/licenses/by-sa/2.5/deed.en

- Creative Commons Attribution-Share Alike 2.0 Generic (CC BY-SA 2.0): http://creativecommons.org/licenses/by/2.0/deed.en http://creativecommons.org/publicdomain/zero/1.0/deed.en

- Creative Commons Attribution-Share Alike 1.0 Generic (CC BY-SA 1.0): http://creativecommons.org/licenses/by-sa/1.0/deed.en

- CC0 1.0 Universal (CC0 1.0) Public Domain Dedication (CC0 1.0)

- GNU Free Documentation License (GFDL): http://en.wikipedia.org/wiki/Wikipedia:Text_of_the_GNU_Free_Documentation_License

Timespinner
Press